YOUR KNOWLEDGE H

Bibliographic information published by the German National Library:

The German National Library lists this publication in the National Bibliography; detailed bibliographic data are available on the Internet at http://dnb.dnb.de .

Imprint:

Copyright © 2008 GRIN Verlag, Open Publishing GmbH
Print and binding: Books on Demand GmbH, Norderstedt Germany
ISBN: 9783640533855

This book at GRIN:

http://www.grin.com/en/e-book/141912/the-shadow-economy-a-critical-analysis

Dennis Ducke, Gabor Ivanyi, Mark Kan

The Shadow Economy – A Critical Analysis

GRIN Publishing

GRIN - Your knowledge has value

Since its foundation in 1998, GRIN has specialized in publishing academic texts by students, college teachers and other academics as e-book and printed book. The website www.grin.com is an ideal platform for presenting term papers, final papers, scientific essays, dissertations and specialist books.

Visit us on the internet:

http://www.grin.com/

http://www.facebook.com/grincom

http://www.twitter.com/grin_com

Fachhochschule
für Oekonomie & Management
University of Applied Sciences

Fachhochschule für Oekonomie & Management Essen

Study Program

Master of Business Administration

1st Academic Semester 2008

General Economics

Assignment II

"The Shadow Economy – A Critical Analysis"

Authors:

Dennis Ducke

Gabor Ivanyi

Mark Kan

Essen, 28 July 2008

EXECUTIVE SUMMARY

According to the "Focus" magazine approximately 13 million Germans contributed to the shadow economy in 2006! The estimations of Friedrich Schneider, one distinguished expert in this area, showed that the extent of the shadow economy in Germany in 2007 was about 349 billion Euros, which equals to 14.7 percent of Germany's gross domestic product (GDP)!

The scope of the present assignment is to provide an all-embracing and critical overview of the shadow economy, to introduce the main causes, effects and dimensions of the shadow economy and to find answer the question how shadow activities can be limited.

In this context the hidden sector can be defined as all economic activities that are not recorded in the national accounts, but normally should be a part of them and be included in GDP. These actions can be on the one hand absolutely legal in the self-sufficient economy like do-it-your-self, neighbourhood help, but on the other hand completely illegal activities like dealing with drugs and smuggling as well as legal activities, which are illegally being carried out, e.g. tax evasion or illicit work.

The main and most vital reasons for the existence and constant growth of the shadow economy are high taxes or social security contributions burden and the intensity of state regulations. But also sociological-psychological causes like subjective perception of tax burden, falling society values, a bad tax morale and declining loyalty towards the state can have a tremendous impact on the size of the hidden economy.

But is the shadow economy a threat to the official sector? At first glance, the question whether the shadow economy is dangerous might appear strange. However, there are several controversial opinions about this matter. The analysis of the effects caused by the existence and the growth of the shadow economy is a contradictory topic. The present assignment characterizes the main negative, e.g. distortion of official economic statistics, lower tax revenues and positive effects, e.g. price stabilization, creation of new jobs of the shadow economy and their influence on the national economy.

Following this, the study presents the most popular methods of measuring the shadow economy: direct methods that are mostly based on surveys, the indirect ones that attempt to quantify shadow economic activities by seeking traces left in the official sector and the so-called model approach, which tries to determine the hidden economy by correlating different indicators and statistical variables. Based on the currency demand approach the study provides an overview about the extent of the shadow economy in 21 OECD countries and in Germany.

How to limit the size of the shadow economy? It is suggested to combat its causes throughout reforms of the tax and social security systems and the deregulation of markets instead of acting against the symptoms by punitive measures, intensified controls and stricter labour regulations.

In summary, the shadow economy has become an inseparable subsystem of the official sector with high growth rates of five to seven percent. It has evolved into an important economic factor and has doubtlessly a significant influence on every sector of the national economy. The shadow economy should be considered as a necessary evil and its extent as an indicator of governmental success or failure in economic policy. Hence, the shadow economy must be taken into account by policy makers in their decision making with regards to the official sector.

TABLE OF CONTENTS

LIST OF ABBREVIATIONS

cf.	confer
i.e.	that is
e.g.	exempli gratia
elect.	electrical
EMNID	TNS EMNID GmbH & Co. KG
fig.	figure
GDP	gross domestic product
GNP	gross national product
HRM	Human Resources Management
OECD	Organisation for Economic Cooperation and Development
p.	page
VAT	value added tax

LIST OF FIGURES

1   INTRODUCTION

Shadow economic and do-it-yourself activities are widely spread and can be observed around the world having a tremendous impact on the official economy. It has reached a magnitude, which makes it an inevitable and considerable economic factor posing a challenge for every government[1]. Institutional failure, high taxation and market regulations are alleged to be the main reasons for individuals working on the black economy[2].

Consequently, the interest in determine the very causes and the estimation of the size of the shadow economy and related activities have become a scientific ferventness in order to assess the unknown[3].

While the official economy remains static the shadow economy is booming. During the last years the black economy has become a growth industry in Germany with constant growth rates of five to seven percent. The size of the shadow economy in Germany has reached almost 350 billion Euros, which equals to 15 percent of its gross domestic product. It is assumed that more than 13 million people are earning their money on the black economy[4].

Although crucial information on the size of the shadow economy and the effects of the informal sector on the official economy are available, most governments still try to control those activities through education, punishment and prosecution with just little success.

Therefore, the following assignment has two major goals. The first is to provide an all-embracing overview over the topic shadow economy and to critically analyse the causes for the existence of the underground economy. Moreover different scientific approaches

---

[1] Cf. Schneider and Enste 2002, p. 178.
[2] Cf. Bovi 2002, p. 2.
[3] Cf. Torgler and Schneider 2007, p. 2.
[4] Cf. Schäfer 2004, p. 2.

how to measure its size will be elaborated in due course. The second is to censoriously discuss measures to limit the shadow economical activities. In doing so, the authors try to address the German case.

At this point it should be mentioned that the current assignment can only provide a small insight into the wide field of research of the shadow economy. For further information please see the latest publications and research by Schneider[5].

This study consists of seven chapters. After this introduction chapter two deals with the difficult matter of finding a general definition for the shadow economy by applying different explanatory models.

Part three determines the basic reasons for the existence of the shadow economy. The following chapter elaborates on the different economic effects of the black economy on the official sector, both positive and negative.

Chapter five provides different theoretical approaches to measure the black economy. Based on the currency demand approach estimated results for a large set of OECD countries are being presented. In a second step detailed data on the German case is being presented.

Part six tries to give an answer to the question how the shadow economy can be contained and reduced, providing promising approaches. The conclusion in chapter seven summarizes all findings and will give the finishing touch to the assignment.

---

[5] Cf. Department of Economics 2008, p. 1.

2 WHAT IS THE SHADOW ECONOMY

A variety of names have been created by the English scientific landscape to describe the shadow economy or parts of it using terms like underground economy, hidden, parallel, invisible, black, grey economies, moonlighting or illicit work. A significant number of terms used to characterize the aspects of the shadow economy are also evident in the literature in other languages[6].

Most scientists dealing with the problem of the shadow economy are facing big difficulty in defining it. The following chapter aims to introduce some of the commonly used definitions of this phenomenon as well as to show the main causes and effects of the shadow economy.

2.1 An Approach to Define the Shadow Economy

According to Skolka the shadow economy consists of "(i) Production of goods that is quite legal in itself, but that one or more parties involved try to conceal from the public authorities to avoid paying taxes or similar charges; (ii) production of illegal goods and services; and (iii) concealed income in kind"[7].

Broadly speaking, the shadow economy can be defined as umbrella term for all economic activities that are not recorded in the national accounts for certain reasons but normally should be a part of them and be accounted for in GDP[8].

As shown in figure one, the shadow economy includes absolutely legal activities in the self-sufficient economy like do-it-your-self, neighbourhood help, but also completely illegal activities like prostitution, dealing with drugs and smuggling as well as legal activities, which are illegally being carried out, e.g. tax evasion or illicit work.

---

[6] Cf. Smith 1986, p. 6.
[7] Skolka 1987, p. 35.
[8] Cf. Smith 1986, p. 6-9.

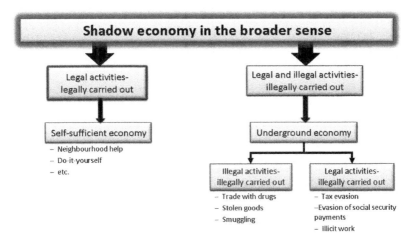

Fig. 1: Classification of the shadow economy (cf. Schneider et al. 2002, p. 12)

The main focus of the present study lies on the illegally carried out legal activities like illicit work (moonlighting), offering illegal employment as well as the evasion of taxes and social security contributions.

2.2 Theoretical Explanatory Models

In the present paragraph two popular explanatory models are introduced trying to explain the micro-economical theoretical reasons why people act in the shadow economy. The authors of the study will present the theory of time allocation and the model of tax evasion.

2.2.1 Model of time allocation

Why do people engage in the shadow economy? The theory of the allocation of time elaborated 1965 by the American scientist Gary Becker considers time as a scarce good. As shown in figure two, an individual makes a decision about an effective distribution of time to be spending either working or with leisure time.

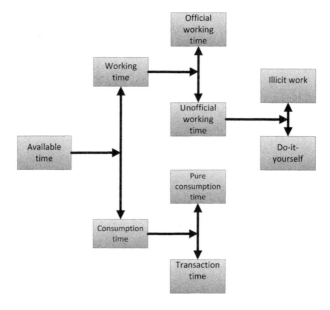

Fig. 2: Time allocation (cf. Schneider et al. 2002, p. 17)

In case the job opportunities in the official sector are not attractive any more for an individual it can decide to spend more time in leisure and to abandon earning money. If an individual is not ready to abandon a higher income, it will start to work in the underground economy - resulting in less free time but more money. Another conclusion is that employees with shorter length of working time have more preparedness to act in the underground economy than people who work overtime[9].

2.2.2 Model of tax evasion

The second approach, which explains activities in the shadow economy and analyses tax evasion behaviour, is the theory of tax evasion. The theory assumes that the individual's decision whether to avoid paying taxes or not is rest upon a rational cost-benefit calculation. According to this theoretical model, tax evasion has potential benefits and costs. Saving money by evading taxes is such a potential benefit. On the other hand,

---

[9] Cf. Schneider and Enste 2002, p. 67.

there are also other potential costs like the risk of being spotted and punished or even arrested.

It is supposed that the taxpayers weight up the costs of evasion, i.e. the risk to be caught against the saving of money. The higher the potential benefits and the lower the risk of detection, the more probably a taxpayer will attempt to evade taxes[10].

---

[10] Cf. Smith 1986, p. 25-28.

3   MAIN CAUSES FOR THE SHADOW ECONOMY

The existence and the development of the shadow economy are caused by various factors that can be partially explained based on the theoretical considerations described in the previous chapter. The most cited and doubtlessly important factors are the increase of tax and social security contributions burden, the raise of the number of governmental regulation in the official sector as well as the reduction of the length of working time. A high unemployment rate and the decrease of people's income levels and wealth also contribute to the black economy[11].

But also sociological-psychological causes like subjective perception of tax and social security contributions, a bad tax morale caused by the changes in society's values and a declining loyalty towards the state or the so-called snowball effect (if nearly everyone does it, why can not I do it also?) are responsible for the growth of shadow economical activities. The sociological-psychological approach, while analyzing the factors influencing the increase of the shadow economy is absolutely necessary, as economic factors alone can only partly explain the growth[12].

The results of 15 empirical studies are shown in figure three confirming that the increase of tax burden, the intensity of state regulations and falling tax morale are the three main driving forces into the shadow economy.

---

[11] Cf. Enste and Schneider 2000, p. 83.
[12] Cf. ebd., p. 77.

Causes	Impact on the increase of the shadow economy
(1) Increased taxes and social security contributions	35-38%
(2) Intensity of state regulations	8-10%
(3) Social transfers	5-7%
(4) Specific labor market regulation	5-7%
(5) Public sector services	5-7%
(6) Tax morale	22-25%
Total	**76-94%**

Fig. 3: Main causes of the increase of the shadow economy (cf. Schneider 2006a, p. 14)

In the following the authors will give a brief overview of some of the above mentioned influencing factors.

3.1 Increase of Tax and Social Security Contribution Burdens

According to most studies on the shadow economy the increase of tax and social security contributions burden is, not surprisingly, one of the main causes for the growth of the informal sector since taxes distort the decision between labour and leisure time.

The bigger the discrepancy between the labour costs in the official sector and the after-tax income of employees, the bigger is the employees' motivation to compensate a loss of income by working in the shadow economy or evading taxes. Since the size of the total labour costs is mainly determined by the costly social security system and the growing tax burden, they can be considered as key factors for the existence and the increase of the shadow economy[13].

How to combat tax evasion and illicit work caused by constantly increasing tax and social security contributions burden? A possible solution could be to reform the taxation system and to decrease the tax level. The lower the tax level, the lower the willingness

---

[13] Cf. Enste and Schneider 2000, p. 83.

of people to engage in the shadow economy or to hide their earnings. A frequent opinion is that tax reductions can lead to increased tax revenues and more employment in the official economy (for a detailed analysis see chapter six)[14].

3.2 Density of Governmental Regulations

The higher the intensity of state regulations, the larger the sizes of the shadow economy! The density of state regulations, especially of labour regulations, is another important factor held responsible for the growth of shadow economical activities.

The density of regulations can be measured by the amount of labour market regulations, wage laws, trade barriers or working restrictions for foreigners. State regulations minimize the freedom of choice and lead to a significant increase of ancillary labour costs. As major components of these costs are shifted onto employees, it motivates individuals who work in the official sector to engage in the shadow economy, where these costs can be avoided.

Governmental regulations as well as state interventions on the economy, e.g. in forms of price dictates or controls, opening hours laws or master craftsmen's diploma, provide also a strong incentive for companies to act illegally[15].

Studies of Johnson, Kaufmann and Schleifer (1997) and Friedman, Johnson, Kaufmann, Zoido-Lobaton (1999) as well as empirical analysis supporting these studies show that countries with a higher density of economical regulation usually have a bigger share of the shadow economy in the total GDP[16]. The increasing number of state regulations is the main reason for the burden placed on companies and individuals dragging people into the underground economy.

---

[14] Cf. Mitchell 2003, p. 83.
[15] Cf. Bühn et al. 2007, p. 10.
[16] Cf. Enste and Schneider 2000, p. 86.

The results of the studies intimate that the state should pay more attention to the improving enforcement of laws and regulations, rather than increasing their numbers[17].

3.3 Unemployment and Reduction of Official Working Hours

Based on the model of time allocation described in chapter 2.2 one can conclude that the reduction in working time as well as unemployment or the possibility of early retirement creates free time for an engagement in the unofficial sector. Also part-time jobs, which are usually paid badly, are putting individuals into a position, where they have to earn additional money by adapting to a second job in the untaxed unofficial economy.

Several attempts to reduce the official length of working time made by German Labour Unions or the introduction of underpaid part-time jobs by the German state in order to downsize the unemployment missed their aim. The idea behind these attempts was to redistribute the work, which amount is limited.

However, several empirical researches showed that these measures just lead to more unofficial activities. Individuals can decide much too easy to spend their additional free time by working in the underground economy[18].

3.4 Subjective Perception of Tax and Social Security Contributions burden

According to several scientists' opinions (Lamnek, Olbrich, Schäfer) the perception of the tax and social security contributions burden is one reason for tax evasion and illegal labour activities. Surveys with respect to this topic showed that about two-third of Germany's population regards the tax burden as to high. This subjective perception of insufferable burden can easily lead to illicit work and tax evasion[19].

---

[17] Cf. Schneider 2000, p. 20-21.
[18] Cf. Enste and Schneider 2000, p. 87.
[19] Cf. Schneider and Enste 2002, p. 93.

3.5 Tax Morale

Another central reason for illegal labour activities is the bad tax morality or in other words a negative attitude of citizens towards the state and taxation. This attitude can be influenced by the perceived tax burden described in the previous chapter. As several studies evidence about 80 percent of the Germans in 1997 and about 87 percent of the population in Germany in 1999 considered the German tax system as unfair. Surveys and assessments of tax morality further showed that the majority of the population does not regard evasion of taxes as a serious crime. On the contrary, people avoiding taxes are often seen as clever businessmen[20].

Figure four shows the influence of social norms and values on the attitude of individuals towards illicit work, tax evasion and social security fraud:

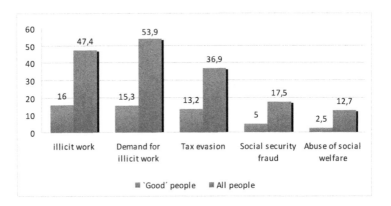

Fig. 4: Willingness to work illicitly, evade taxes and abuse the system in % of people polled (Schneider and Enste 2002, p. 152)

Several scientists state that the shift in values of the society can be clearly seen on the demographical level[21]. Accordingly, younger generations tend more to supply or demand illicit work and evade paying taxes than older ones[22].

---

[20] Cf. Schneider and Enste 2002, p. 93.

[21] Cf. ebd., p. 82.

[22] Cf. ebd., p. 151.

In this context figure five illustrates the decrease of the tax morality in the OECD countries between 1960 and 1978:

Development of the tax morale (%) (the higher the value, the lower the tax morale, i.e., the higher the tax immorality)

Country	1960	1965	1970	1975	1978	Difference 1960-78
Belgium	7,1	8,6	11,6	13,7	14,0	+6,9
Denmark	2,2	2,7	3,6	4,2	4,4	+2,2
Germany	5,5	6,7	9,0	10,6	10,9	+5,4
Finland	2,2	2,7	3,6	4,2	4,4	+2,2
France	8,7	10,6	14,3	16,9	17,3	+8,6
Great Britain	2,2	2,7	3,6	4,2	4,4	+2,2
Ireland	3,8	4,7	6,3	7,4	7,6	+3,8
Italy	10,4	12,6	17,0	20,1	20,6	+10,2
Japan	3,8	4,7	6,3	7,4	7,6	+3,8
Canada	3,8	4,7	6,3	7,4	7,6	+3,8
Netherlands	5,5	6,7	9,0	10,6	10,9	+5,4
Norway	2,2	2,7	3,6	4,2	4,4	+2,2
Austria	5,5	6,7	9,0	10,6	10,9	+5,4
Sweden	2,2	2,7	3,6	4,2	4,4	+2,2
Switzerland	0,6	0,7	1,0	1,2	1,2	+0,6
Spain	7,1	8,6	11,6	13,7	14,0	+6,9
USA	3,8	4,7	6,3	7,4	7,6	+3,8

Fig. 5: The tax morale as an influencing factor for the rise of the shadow economy (Schneider and Enste 2002, p. 152)

This attempt to quantify the influence of falling tax morality demonstrates that especially in Italy, France, Belgium, Spain, but also in Germany, the willingness of people to work illicitly has grown tremendously over the past 30 years.

4   EFFECTS OF THE SHADOW ECONOMY

Is the shadow economy harmful? The analysis of the effects caused by the existence and the growth of the shadow economy is a contradictory topic. At first glance, the question whether the shadow economy might be dangerous or not appears strange. However, there are some controversial opinions about it. This chapter will try to differentiate the different positive and negative effects of the shadow economy and its influence on the official sector.

One often-instanced main negative effect is the distortion of official economic statistics:

- wrong sized GDP, as the real added value is much higher than the measured one
- wrong calculation of the economic growth rate as the increase of production capacities in the shadow economy is not recorded
- too high inflation rates, if assumed that that the prices rise in the unofficial sector is more slowly than in the official economy
- wrong calculation of the unemployment rate since there are less unemployed people than assumed

Such distortions of statistical indicators can result in wrong economic-political decisions[23].

Another widespread opinion is that the shadow economy leads to lower tax revenues of the state, raises the state deficit, jeopardizes the social and medical insurance systems, slows down the country's economic growth and increases the unemployment rate. Necessary public investments, e.g. on education and infrastructure cannot be done due to the lack of financing. Public goods and services cannot be offered in the required quantity and quality[24].

---

[23] Cf. Schneider and Enste 2002, p. 170.
[24] Cf. Schäfer 2004, p. 13.

Furthermore, there are several negative welfare effects influencing the honest taxpayers in the official economy. They have to bare higher labour costs, tax burdens and comply with numerous state regulations whereas people engaged in the unofficial sector can avoid these costs[25].

Companies in the shadow economy can offer their goods and services much cheaper than firms in the official sector because of tax evasion. Thus, it makes the goods produced in the official sector not competitive and lead to a decline in demand and sales. Honest businesses might be pushed out of the market or forced to act illegally if their competitors in the underground sector offer similar or substitute goods or services[26].

However, there are several weighty positive counterarguments that are contrary to the mentioned negative considerations. The statement that the shadow economy causes a reduction in state tax revenues and limits financial resources of the social security system might be only conditionally true. The reason being is that a considerable part of value added in the unofficial economy is created, because of more favorable conditions in the shadow sector. In other words, this added value might not have been created at all or not to the same extent, if less favorable conditions would have been existed in the official economy. Hence, it is not correct to talk about a real tax deficit.

The decline in demand in the official economy is compensated by an increase of demand and added value in the shadow economy. Hence, there is just a shift in demand from one sector to the other and not a real decline. Moreover, it is estimated that more than 70 percent of incomes earned in the shadow economy are spend on the official economy, which results in extra consumption and additional taxes[27].

---

[25] Cf. Schneider and Enste 2002, p. 172.
[26] Cf. ebd., p. 163.
[27] Cf. Schäfer 2004, p. 13.

Higher consumption and hidden activities lead to growing production in the shadow economy providing new jobs for both, individuals with higher qualification and low skills.

Another positive effect of the shadow economy is the so-called price stabilization effect. Low prices in the unofficial sector lead to more favourable prices and a boost competition in the official economy.

Finally, the underground economy is often considered as a response to and an escape from overregulated markets, high tax burdens and as a reaction against too much state control. In this context the shadow economy is supposed to lead to more competition and an increased efficiency. Existing inefficiencies and distortions in the official static markets can be partly corrected by the pressure and dynamic of the more flexible shadow sector resulting in a meaningful allocation of resources in the national economy[28].

---

[28] Cf. Schäfer 2004, p. 13-14.

5   THE DIMENSION OF THE SHADOW ECONOMY

To highlight the dimension of the shadow economy it is indispensable to develop
methods to estimate the size of the shadow economy. Different theoretical and practical
orientated methods are shortly presented in the first paragraph. Afterwards in chapter
5.2 the value of the black economy in the 21 OECD countries is being compared. The
historical development of Germany's black economy and its allocation in different
sections will conclude this chapter.

5.1   Methods to Estimate the Size of the Shadow Economy

The biggest problem and the weakness of all different models is the question how to
quantify something that is hidden in the shadow? As a matter of fact nobody, who is
working on the black economy, would like to voluntarily provide information on his
illegal activities and to get punished the same time. Consequently, they try to hide their
actions. But these illegal actions leave traces in certain areas of the official sector. And
just because of these traces it is possible to develop methods and analytic models to
estimates the size of the shadow economy.

In figure six an overview of the most common statistical and scientific methods is
given. It must be pointed out that due to the lack of usable information and existing
characteristics of the shadow economy no "best" method can be selected. Each model
has got its strength and weaknesses but a zero forecast uncertainty can not be assured[29].

---

[29] Cf. Schönfelder 1998, p. 34.

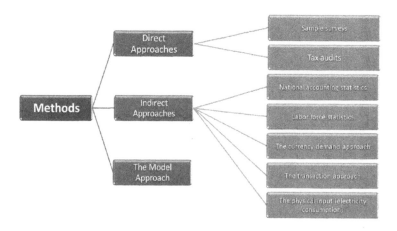

Fig. 6: Estimation methods (own figure)

The direct, indirect and the so-called model approach are the most common estimation methods to measure the size of the shadow economy. Direct methods are mostly based on various surveys. By contrast indirect approaches try to quantify shadow economic activities by seeking traces left in the official sector. Besides that the model approach tries to determine the hidden economy by correlating different indicator and statistical variables[30].

5.1.1 Direct approaches

5.1.1.1 Sample surveys

The sample surveys are based on well-designed surveys and rely on voluntary replies. Persons engaged in the informal economy are naturally reluctant and not willing to provide the desired information by trying to keep a low profile in public. Responses, which are based on voluntary information, must therefore be critical examined and handled, because they are very sensitive in nature. To gather utilizable results all questions must be carefully selected and the privacy of the respondents is paramount[31].

---

[30] Cf. Schneider 2004, p. 101.
[31] Cf. Enste and Schneider 2002, p. 9.

The main advantages of surveys are detailed information on the structure of activities and the nature of employment[32].

5.1.1.2 Tax audit method

The tax audit method tries to detect shadow economical activities by analysing the discrepancies between declared and real income. To detect tax evasion, the financial authorities select samples of persons and force them on pain of penalties to declare their real taxable income. From the differences between declared tax and the real income the tax auditing method can estimate the size of the shadow economy. The problem of this method is that the persons for the sample are not selected randomly, but who are more likely to be subject to tax evasion. Consequently, the findings are not representative for the total population[33].

5.1.2 Indirect approaches

5.1.2.1 Discrepancy between national expenditure and income statistics

This method estimates the size of the shadow economy on basis of the differences between income and expenditure statistics taken from the national accounting data. In the national accounting the earnings degree of GNP should be equal to the expenditure of GNP. The gap between the expenditure measure and the income measures can be used as an indicator for the dimension of the shadow economy. The grade of accuracy is increasing if more money is spent by the respective population than taken. One negative aspect of this method is that all errors that slipped into the calculation of GNP are causing an error within the statistics and consequently in the calculation of the hidden economy. Therefore such estimates are creating only a poor and not very reliable picture of the shadow economical activities in the selected country[34].

5.1.2.2 Discrepancy between official and actual labour force

A decrease in participation of the labour force in the official economy can be understood as an indicator for a growing shadow economical activity. In this model the differences between the constant assumed labour force and the real participation is an

---

[32] Cf. Schneider 2006a, p. 36.
[33] Cf. Schneider et al. 2002, p. 23.
[34] Cf. Schneider 2006a, p. 40.

indicator for the black economy. The negative aspect of this method is that the participation rate can heavily differentiate due to other reasons, which have not their seeds in the shadow economy. For example, an employee in the unofficial sector can also be employed in the official sector[35].

5.1.2.3 The transactions approach

This method is based on the idea, that a stable relation over time between the dimension of transaction and official GNP is existing. Below displayed set phrase is used for the calculation:

$$M*V=p*T$$

Variable	Value
M	Money
V	Velocity
p	Price
T	Total transaction

The transaction approach uses the data of the overall amount of monetary transactions in an economy to estimate the entire nominal GDP (unofficial plus official). In a second step the value of the black economy is being assessed by subtracting official GDP from total nominal GDP. This method is generally attractive, but very difficult to apply, because the values are hard to itemize. To generate a representative picture of the shadow economy a relatively high amount of empirical data is required to avoid bias, caused by legal cross payments that have no origin in the black economy[36].

---

[35] Cf. Schneider 2006, p. 41.
[36] Cf. ebd., 41-42.

5.1.2.4 The currency demand approach

Similar to the transaction approach the currency demand method tries to derive the size of the shadow economy from the development of the currency demand[37]. It is based on the theory that activities and services in the shadow economy are mostly paid in cash, without leaving any or only very few traces behind. If the need for currency is increasing in a fixed period deviating from the base year, it can be an indication for the existence of shadow economical actions[38].

The currency demand approach uses these thoughts and reasons by taking the differences between the real growth of the currency demand and the "normal" growth of the currency demand of the shadow economy into account. Any unexplainable increase in the demand for cash, which can not be attributed to conventional payments, e.g. increasing income, payment habits or interest rate, is accounted for the hidden economy.

One major disadvantage of this method is that not all activities in the shadow economy are paid in cash. Some services may be shelled out with checks or paid in kind, which would lead to a distortion of the estimations[39].

5.1.2.5 The physical input (electricity consumption) method

The Physical inputs method is striving to compare the dynamics between electricity consumption and GDP. It estimates the growth of the black economy from the electricity usage assuming that electricity consumption is the most excellent and single physical indicator of all true economic activities. By subtracting the growth rate of official GDP from the growth rate of overall electricity usage the difference in growth can be attributed to the informal sector. The weakness of this method is the fact, that not all activities in the shadow economy require a constant amount of electricity and the type of the energy source is not fixed. For example, commodities like gas or oil could also be used for power generation. Furthermore, the present increase in electrical efficiency also tampers the comparison of both dynamics[40].

---

[37] Cf. Schönfelder 1998, p. 38.
[38] Cf. Enste 2003, p. 19.
[39] Cf. Enste and Schneider 2002, p. 18-22.
[40] Cf. Enste and Schneider 2000, p. 96.

5.1.3 The model approach

The model approach attempts to estimate the size of the shadow economy as a function of observed variables and indicators for the hidden economy. The basic principle of this approach is that the unofficial sector is not influenced by different determinants, but itself manipulates general economic indictors of the official economy. In this context resulting cash payments from the burden of taxations might be a possible correlating variable that can be used to develop a sustainable model.

The complexity of this method, which considers multiple causes and effects, is its biggest advantage and disadvantage at the same time[41].

5.2   The Size of the Shadow Economy in the 21 OECD Countries

In the following paragraphs the size of the shadow economy in the 21 OECD countries will be analyzed applying the currency demand approach, one of the most commonly used approaches by economists[42]. The magnitude of the shadow economy in the subsequent charts is displayed in percentage of GDP. The data is based on Prof. Dr. Friedrich Schneider's calculation from 2008[43].

In figure seven the size of the black economy in the 21 OCED countries and the average within the OECD is shown:

---

[41] Cf. Enste and Schneider 2002, p. 8.
[42] Cf. Schneider 2000b, p. 8.
[43] Cf. Schneider 2008, p. 14-24.

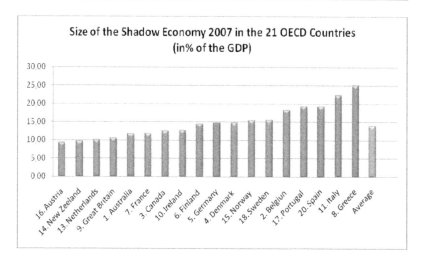

Fig. 7: Size of the shadow economy in the 21 OECD countries (cf. Schneider 2008, p.22)

It is noticeable that countries in southern Europe like Italy, Spain, Portugal or Greek have a higher percentage of shadow economy than others. This could be explained by a larger rate of corruption[44], a higher rate of unemployment or a lower tax moral, unlike the average[45]. Germany, with an estimated value of 14.7 percent of its GDP is in center field. This is slightly higher than the average of 13.3 percent and comparable to the Nordic countries.

If one casts a critical eye on the development of the shadow economy in the OECD countries over time as displayed in figure eight, it will become obvious, that the hidden economy is slightly decreasing overall. It dropped down by an average of 3.5 percent from 2000 to 2008.

---

[44] Cf. Ernste and Schneider, 2000, p. 32.
[45] Cf. Dreher 2006, p. 14.

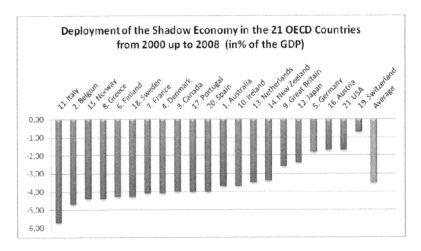

Fig. 8:Deployment of the shadow economy in the 21 OECD countries from 2000 up to 2008 (cf. Schneider 2008, p. 23)

The reasons for this deployment are miscellanous measures launched by the OECD countries to enforce a meanigful economic policy capable of combating hidden activities. But moreover, the economic boom in Central Europe resulting in a reduction of unemployment is playing a big role in the decrease of the unofficial economy. Besides that, also the beginning deregulation troughout the EU is starting to take effect[46].

In spite of the overall decline, the shadow economical activities in Germany are nearly unchanged and stagnating on a high level. One likely reason for this can be explained by the raise of the value added tax in the year 2007 from 16 to 19 percent, the abolishment of the subsidy for the promotion of hous building or the incrase of health insurance contributuion in the year 2007[47]. Furthermore, Germany still belongs to the countries within the OECD with one of highest regulation densities.

---

[46] More measure will be identified and explained at length in chapter six.
[47] Cf. Schneider 2008, p. 5.

5.3 The Size of the Shadow Economy in Germany

As already described in the previous chapter, Germany's shadow economy is considerably high. In figure nine the historical development of the shadow economy is visualized.

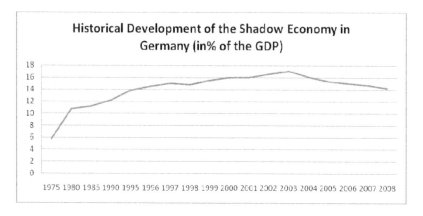

Fig. 9: Historical development of the shadow economy in Germany (cf. Schneider 2008, p. 16)

Since 1975 the black economy rapidly grew from about 6 percent up to 16.5 percent of GDP in 2003. In the last 30 years it remained constantly on a high stage. One reason for this high rate can bee seen in the decreasing tax moral[48], the permanently growing unemployment, the intensity of state regulation[49], the increase of direct and indirect tax burdens and Germany' bureaucracy[50].

After reaching its peak in 2003 the shadow economy has been slightly decreasing up to now. This might be positive consequence of the evaluation of the mini job settlement in 2003 and the EU wide economic boost in the last five years[51].

---

[48] Cf. Schneider 2006, p. 13.
[49] Cf. Enste and Hardege 2007, p. 8-10.
[50] Cf. Bühn et al. 2007, p. 9-11.
[51] Cf. Schneider 2008, p. 2.

Not only the magnitude of the hidden sector in Germany, but also its segmentation by sectors is quite interesting to observe. The pie chart in figure ten illustrate the main focus areas of shadow economical activities in Germany.

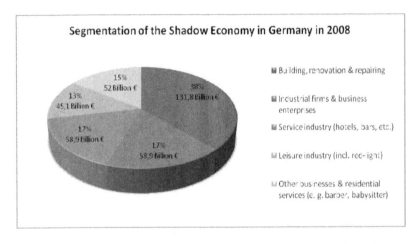

Fig. 10: Segmentation of the shadow economy in Germany in 2008 (cf. Schneider 2008, p. 17)

Not very suprisingly, the biggest proportion with 38 percent is made up by the building, renovation and repairing sector, followed by industrial firms and business enterprises. The service industry, e.g. hotels, bars and restaurants are holding a share of 17 percent in the shadow economical activities in Germany. But also the leisure industry including the red light districts and gambling sector are generating a considerably turn-over of 45.1 billion Euros in the hidden economy. This corresponds to a percentage of 13 percent. Other businesses and residential services like barbers, babysitters or pizza delivery services were exchanging 52 billion Euros in illicit earning in 2008. Alltogehter, the overall size of the shadow economy in Germany equaled to 15 percent of GDP in 2008[52].

---

[52] Cf. Schneider 2008, p. 17.

On top of the above outlined segmentation, figure eleven pictures the building industry in Germany, which is the biggest and simoultaneusly most labour intesive service of the unofficial economy, subdevided by sectors.

Fig. 11: Segmentation of the shadow economy in Germany in 2008 into the building sector and the trade and repair business (cf. Schneider 2008, p. 18)

Unsuprisingly, the main construction and secondary contract work with a total of 80.4 billion Euros in 2008 are the two major contributors to the hidden economy. More than 46 billion Euros were approximatly earned in the main constuction trade equaling a percentage of 35 percent and 34.4 billion Euros by secondary contract work with a share of 26 percent. 27.7 billion Euros were illicitly generated by trade and repair businesses in construction (21 percent) and 23.7 billion Euros in so-called other repair services for elect. euipment and domestic appliances[53].

---

[53] Cf. Schneider 2008, p. 18.

6 MEASURE FOR LIMITING THE SHADOW ECONOMY

After the effects and the dimensions of shadow economical activities have been discussed in the previous chapters, the following section tries to describe the basic procedures of how to limit or reduce moonlighting. Firstly, the benefit of actions for combating the black economy in Germany by applying stricter state control will be briefly described. Secondly, different economic policy recommendations, based on the reasons for the shadow economy that have been described in chapter two, will be discussed at length.

6.1 Cost-benefit Analysis of Combating Black Economy in Germany by Stricter State Control

Although, the reasons for and economic consequences of the black economy on the official sector in Germany are tremendous and being discussed for almost the last 50 years in ratifying existing and introducing new laws[54], most politicians and bureaucrats still tend to contain moonlighting by combating its symptoms and enforcing stricter controls and legislations[55].

Starting in 1957 violations of the "law to combat illegal employment" are being punished, since 1975 treated as misdemeanour and since August 2002 punished with fines up to 300.000 Euros, in cases of illegal employment with fines of up to 500.000 Euros[56]. From August 2004 on the federal cabinet decided to treat black labour no longer as a misdemeanour but as a criminal offence. In the same breath the sole responsibility for action has been shifted from the federal employment office to the customs authority by increasing the number of posts to 7.000 in total. This led to an increase in personnel cost by 50 percent or a total of 500 million Euros in the year 2004[57].

---

[54] Cf. Bundesrechnungshof 2008, p 8-10.
[55] Cf. Enste and Hardege 2007, p 7.
[56] Cf. Enste 2003, p. 8.
[57] Cf. Bundesministerium der Finanzen 2004, p. 83; Enste 2003, p. 8.

Even though a drastic correctional intensification and a simultaneously increase in labour utilisation could have been observed in the past years, less preliminary proceeding have been initiated. Figure twelve displays the relation between imposed fines and actually paid fines and moreover the size of the shadow economy and the labour cost and cost for criminal prosecution.

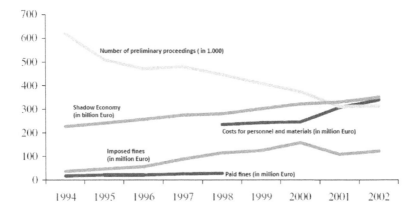

Fig. 12: Cost-value ratio of the abetment of the shadow economy in Germany (cf. Enste and Schneider 2005, p. 17)

Albeit the expenses for criminal prosecution of moonlighting are constantly raising the shadow economy only started to decrease slowly after 2003. Besides that, the amount of actually paid fines has not changed. Every effort in reducing the size of the shadow economy by either higher fines or prosecution had almost zero effect[58]. In summary one can say that only every thousandth illicit worker, a high chance of recovery provided, is paying a fine. Political measures, which only intensify state control, can only combat the symptoms for moonlighting but not the causes[59]. From a cost-benefit perspective the fighting of the symptoms has failed and is not a suitable way to contain shadow economic activities, which are still on the rise. Long-term incentives that try to enforce

[58] Cf. Enste 2003, p. 8-10.
[59] Cf. Schneider 2004, p. 84.

a meaningful economic order, improve the tax moral and the identification of the citizens with state actions seem to be more promising[60].

6.2 General Economic Policy Recommendations

Manifold reasons for working on and the existence of the black economy can be found and have been detailed described in chapter two. Considering the fact, that increasing moonlighting is just seen as a peccadillo and as a kind of valve of the small man against a too high tax burden and fiscal waste, appeals and sharper state controls to prevent illegal work appear to make only little sense (see paragraph 6.1)[61].

Therefore, the major task must be to find measures for limiting the shadow economy by general economic policy recommendations, which trigger the previously delineated reasons like tax and duty burdens or the density of regulations of the labour market. Figure 13 summarizes the most important suggestions:

Fig. 13: General economic policy recommendations (cf. Schneider and Enste 2002, p. 182)

---

[60] Cf. Enste 2003, p. 16.
[61] Cf. Schäfer 2004, p. 14.

6.2.1 Reduction of tax and social security burdens

Reducing the tax rates and social security burdens significantly is the key recommendation to limit illicit work[62]. Empiric studies show that the average handcraft hourly earnings in the official sector are three timesw higher than on the black economy. In other words: a normal wage earner has to work almost four hours to "afford" a one-hour handcraft service[63]. By reducing the gap between gross and disposable income the attractiveness to work on the black economy and the motivation can be reduced in due course. In summary a drastically reductions of labour cost would not only result in improved performance, but would also shift productivity towards the official economy[64].

Besides efforts to reduce above-mentioned burdens, one possible way to limit shadow economical activities is to relief low-income earners from non-wage labour costs. The higher the income level for low-income earners and the lower the flat rates for security burdens are, the more effective the movement of labour towards the shadow economy can be detained[65]. When Germany first curbed the possibilities to start low-income employment it resulted in more illicit work in 1999[66]. On the other hand the reintroduction of the expanded "Mini-Jobs", which came into force 1 April 2003, resulted in a decline of the shadow economy by approximately nine billion Euros in the following years[67].

Another way to shift supply over to the official sector is not only to reduce non-wage labour cost, but also to limit value added taxes (VAT) for labour intensive work like handcraft and related services. This proposal is also know as the Luxembourg Model. For example Luxembourg, France and other European countries are already exercising this model, which can be put on the same level with the utilization of reduced VAT rates[68].

---

[62] Cf. Enste and Hardege 2007, p. 7.
[63] Cf. Schneider et al. 2002, p. 73.
[64] Cf. Schäfer 2004, p. 14-16.
[65] Cf. ebd., p. 17.
[66] Cf. Enste 2002, p. 202-203.
[67] Cf. Schneider 2006b, p. 102.
[68] Cf. Schneider 2007, p. 176.

Although, those recommendations would result in reduced state revenues it is more important that the creation of value is achieved in the official economy[69].

6.2.2 Reduction of density of regulations

As mentioned earlier in chapter two, government regulations and labour market regulations in particular, have a major effect on employers' cost and workers' incentives in the official economy[70].

Especially regulations in Germany are extremely dense, surprisingly focusing on the labour-intensive service sector with hundreds of laws, provisions and guidelines. In this context and in order to stop the movement of labour to the hidden economy, collective agreements on working conditions like working time agreements and the protection against unlawful dismissal must be examined. Thus market exit restrictions that are inflexible in case of dismissal are market entry barriers for workers seeking employment[71].

Furthermore, market entry restrictions and prohibitions for the employment of foreigners, but also the necessity of the German so-called "Meisterbrief" must be reassessed. Without this necessity more and even foreign EU craftsmen could offer services in the official sector, which would have been impossible with the prerequisite of the foreman's certificate. Although first promising steps towards the abolishment of the master craftsman's diploma can be witnessed, it is only a small step towards the phase-out of regulations[72].

Especially the transition to flexible working hours must be achieved in order to minimise shadow economic activities. An empirical EMNID study in 1997 came to the result that for only 40 percent of the employees the agreed working time corresponded

---

[69] Cf. Schäfer 2004, p. 17-18.
[70] Cf. Enste 2003, p. 16.
[71] Cf. Schäfer 2004, p. 19.
[72] Cf. Schneider and Enste 2002, p. 138-141.

with the desired one. Moreover, 27 percent of all individuals wished to work even longer[73].

Every forced working time reduction that is based on a working time policy, leads to an increase in personal leisure time and provides the opportunity to work in the shadow economy. The redistribution of work will only succeed if the reduction of working hours meets the wishes of employees[74].

Therefore, the labour market must be deregulated to give the economy and the market participants a free reign for their businesses. The government must ensure a market environment that addresses the general preferences and the sovereignty of the individuals. Note: every service that cannot be offered in the official sector will be demanded in the black economy.

6.2.3 Allocation of transfer payments

Besides the break up of bureaucracy the right allocation of transfer payments such as welfare, unemployment assistance and unemployment benefit has a severe impact on the shadow economy and can reduce the migration into the unofficial sector. To stop welfare recipients from working illicit and to make them labour in the official economy two conditions must be fulfilled. In the first place, earnings from individuals, who are obtaining redistributive payments, must not be accounted for his welfare payments. Every income that is liable to deduction equals to a 100 percent marginal tax rate on the individual earnings. If 100 percent of his income is being deducted, the incentive to work in the official sector will be practically zero[75].

Secondly, statutory benefits must be combined or limited to the start of work as it has been put before by the so-called Wisconsin-Model[76]. It introduced mandatory workfare

---

[73] Cf. Schäfer 2004, p. 20.
[74] Cf. Schneider et al. 2002, p. 79-80.
[75] Cf. Schneider and Enste 2002, p. 122-124.
[76] Cf. Schäfer 2004, p. 22.

to obtain redistributive payments and marked a significant change in state policy towards aid recipients in Wisconsin-Milwaukee[77].

A similar approach has been undertaken by the federal state of Baden-Württemberg. With the model test of the "Einstiegsgeld in Baden-Württemberg" welfare recipients, who were living on dole for a considerable amount of time, were given an extra financial support for the start of work. Simultaneously, only 50 percent of the gross income was subject to ancillary labour costs. Thus the state tried to motivate pauper to start a job in the official labour market[78].

In summary, the government must a create a foundation in order to stop illicit work, where permanently unemployed-persons have a legal chance to obtain higher incomes if solely working in the official sector, instead of working on the black economy and receiving welfare at the same time. The Wisconsin model or the Baden-Württemberg pilot project could be promising measure to limit the shadow economy by allocating transfer payments in a prudential way.

6.2.4 Consolidation of the public sector

Also the public sector and the public's attitude towards the state play an important role to reduce shadow economic activities. Only if the citizens assume that there interest will be properly presented and that they will receive a service in return for paid taxes, they will be willing to spent more money and taxes on the official economy without drifting into the black economy[79].

Therefore, it is highly important that the state focuses on its main tasks to avoid waste of public revenue. A lean and proactive government against illicit work can be assumed, if the public institutions and administration are smaller and easier to overlook for the individual[80].

---

[77] Cf. Pawasarat and Quinn 2008, p. 1.
[78] Cf. Schneider et al. 2002, p. 76-79.
[79] Cf. Enste and Hardege 2007, p. 8.
[80] Cf. Hösli 2002, p. 109-110.

To support this idea and the willingness to pay tributes, one promising solution is to reinforce the identification with the state and the participation of citizen in the decision making process by strengthening the direct democratic element. In doing so, loyalty towards the public administration can be enforced[81].

---

[81] Cf. Schneider and Enste 2002, p. 151-153.

7   CONCLUSION

This assignment tried to cast some light on the topic of shadow economic activities, ways to appreciatively measure its size and the inevitable effects on the official economy.

Different approaches to define the shadow economy have been introduced and the size of the black economy in some OECD countries and Germany has been determined by using the most common currency demand approach. Based on the different reasons for the appearance of the hidden economy some measures to limit its magnitude have been developed.

In principle, the shadow economy has become a subsystem of the official economy with high growth rates of five to seven percent. Almost 15 percent of the gross domestic product is generated by the black economy. It evolved to an important economic factor and a challenge for today's governments. Therefore, the shadow economy must be taken into account in policy measures seeking to stimulate the official economy – resulting in growth impulse.

Falling economic policy is the driving force for the strong increase in shadow economic activities. A promising economic policy should try to combat its causes instead of curing the symptoms.

To condemn shadow economic activities fewer regulations and lower tax and social security contributions are the most effective way of transferring more activity to the official free market economy. Intensified controls to penalise illicit work and stricter regulations especially in labour intensive work have the opposite effect to the one intended.

In the long run the shadow economy can be referred to as an evolutionary process creating an increasingly dynamic basis forcing marketers to rethink their actions and governments to deregulate and reduce taxes. By this means economic activity could be shifted back by creating an environment that is based on the idea of a free and capable of acting markets.

BIBLIOGRAPHY

BOVI, M. (2002). The nature of the underground economy. Some evidence from OECD countries. Rome: ISAE.

BÜHN, A., KARMANN, A. AND SCHNEIDER, F. (2007). Size and Development of the Shadow Economy and Do-It-Yourself Activities in Germany. CESifo Working Paper No. 2021. June 2007.

BUNDESMINISTERIUM DER FINANZEN (2004). Neues Gesetz zur Intensivierung der Bekämpfung der Schwarzarbeit und damit zusammenhängender Steuerhinterziehung. Monatsbericht 09/2004. Berlin.

BUNDESRECHNUNGSHOF (2008). Bericht nach § 99 BHO über die Organisation und Arbeitsweise der Finanzkontrolle Schwarzarbeit (FKS). Bonn.

DEPARTMENT OF ECONOMICS (2008). Publications/latest research by Dr. Friedrich Schneider. [online]. http://www.econ.jku.at/531/ [Accessed 24 July 2008].

DREHER, A. (2006). Corruption and the Shadow Economy: An Empirical Analysis. CESifo Working Paper No. 1653. January 2006.

ENSTE, D. H. (2002). Schattenwirtschaft und institutioneller Wandel. Tübingen: Mohr Siebeck.

ENSTE, D. H. AND SCHNEIDER, F. (2002). Hiding in the Shadows - The Growth of the Underground Economy. IMF Working Papers - Economic Issues No. 30. March 2002.

ENSTE, D. H. (2003). Ursachen der Schattenwirtschaft in den OECD-Staaten. Iw-trends 4/2003. Institut der Deutschen Wirtschaft Köln.

ENSTE, D. H. AND SCHNEIDER, F. (2005). Schattenwirtschaft und irreguläre Beschäftigung: Irrtümer, Zusammenhänge und Lösungen. Working Paper. June 2005.

ENSTE, D. H. AND HARDEGE, S. (2007). Regulierung und Schattenwirtschaft. Iw-trends 01/2007. Institut der Deutschen Wirtschaft Köln.

ENSTE, D. H. AND SCHNEIDER, F. (2000). Shadow Economies Around the World: Size, Cause and Consequences. IMF Working Paper 00/26. February 2000.

HÖSLI, A. (2002). Schwarzarbeit: Ursachen, Formen, Zusammenhänge und Wirkungen illegaler Beschäftigung sowie Vorschläge zu deren substantieller Bekämpfung.Thesis (doctoral). University Zürich.

MITCHELL, D. J. (2003). The OECD and EU are wrong: Tax competition should be celebrated not persecuted. In: SCHÄDLER, P., MENICHETTI M. ed. Private Banking im Schlaglicht internationaler Regulierungen. Heidelberg: Birkhäuser. 33-47.

PAWASARAT, J. AND QUINN, L. M. (2008). Wisconsin welfare employment experiments: An evaluation of the WEJT and CWEP programs. [online]. http://www.uwm.edu/Dept/ETI/pages/surveys/each/wlss93.htm [Accessed 24 July 2008].

SCHÄFER, W. (2004). Die Schattenwirtschaft bekämpfen! Von der Schattenwirtschaft lernen? Abschlussbericht der Kommission Schattenwirtschaft des Wirtschaftsrats der CDU Hamburg e.V. Hamburg.

SCHNEIDER, F. (2000a). Illegal activities, but still value added ones (?): Size, causes and measurement of the Shadow Economies all over the world. CESifo Working paper No. 305. June 2000.

SCHEIDER, F. (2000b): The Increase of the Size of the Shadow Economy of 18 OECD Countries : Some Preliminary Explanations. CESifo Working Paper No. 306. June 2000.

SCHNEIDER F. AND ENSTE, D. (2002). The Shadow Economy - An International Survey. Cambridge: Cambridge University Press.

SCHNEIDER, F, VOLKER, J. AND CASPAR, S. (2002). Schattenwirtschaft und Schwarzarbeit. Beliebt bei vielen – Problem für Alle. Baden-Baden: Nomos.

SCHNEIDER, F. (2004). Arbeit im Schatten. Wo Deutschlands Wirtschaft wirklich wächst. Wiesbaden: Gabler.

SCHNEIDER, F. (2006a). Shadow Economies and Corruption all over the World: What do we really Know? CESifo Working Paper No. 1806. September 2006.

SCHNEIDER, F. (2006b). The Shadow Economy in Germany: A Blessing or a Curse for the Official Economy? Economic Analysis and Policy (EAP). Vol. 38 No. 1, March 2008. 89-112.

SCHNEIDER, F. (2007). Does the shadow economy pose a challenge to economic and public finance policy? Some preliminary findings. In: BLANKART, C. B., BAKE, P. AND BORCK, R. ed. Public economics and public choice. New York: Springer, 157-180.

SCHEIDER, F. (2008). Leichter (deutlicher) Rückgang der Schattenwirrtschaft in Deutschland. Linz: Johannes Kepler Universität.

SCHÖNFELDER, M. (1998). Schwarzarbeit und Schattenwirtschaft im Baugewerbe. Herausforderung für den Europäischen Markt oder Kampfansage and Gesetzgeber und Tarifsysteme. Thesis (doctoral). Ludwig-Maximilians-University Munich.

SKOLKA, J. (1987). A few facts about the hidden economy. In: ALESSANDRINI, S., DALLAGO, B. ed. The unofficial economy. Vermont: Gower Publishing House. 35-59.

SMITH, S. (1986). Britain's shadow economy. Oxford: University Printing House.

TORGLER, B. AND SCHNEIDER, F. (2007). Shadow Economy, Tax Moral, Governance and Institutional Quality: A Panel Analysis. CESifo Working Paper No. 1923. February 2007.

ITM-CHECKLIST

Main Topic	Reasonable Questions	Recommendations/Comments
General Economics	Which global economical relevance belongs to this topic?	The topic of the assignment is of prime importance in the context of general economics. Especially in Germany and other EU-countries the shadow economy, in particular illicit work and tax evasion, are publicly and controversially discussed themes. Most societies try to decrease the extent of the black economy. An important question is thereby whether it should be combated by punitive measures or rather through reforms of the tax and social security system and deregulating markets.
Strategic Management	How is the strategically relevance of this topic, esp. under competition, resource, risk and sustain?	The shadow economy has doubtlessly a significant influence on every sector of the national economy and is therefore a strategically relevant topic for the whole society. Even though the effects of the shadow economy are not only negative, the necessity to combat the shadow economy is beyond all questions.

Main Topic	Reasonable Questions	Recommendations/Comments
Marketing	Which pro and cons are coming out of the proposals? Esp. for the higher projects, potentials in general for the company? Which action should be taken on the marketing side for further promotion?	Marketing campaigns, educational campaigns and public relations against illicit work and tax evasion can be powerful means of supporting the government to reduce the shadow economy.
Financial Management	Which criteria should be chosen for an appropriate financial concept? Which risks are given and how can they avoided it? How is the impact from external factors?	The fiscal effects of the shadow sector on the national economy of a country should be considered. According to official calculations, only illicit work causes several billions Euro annual tax deficit in Germany. However, these calculations do not take the positive effects of the shadow economy on state tax revenues into account.

Main Topic	Reasonable Questions	Recommendations/Comments
Human Resources Management	Which personnel consequences (quantitative /qualitative) are given by the proposal?	Shadow economy is a matter of importance for the strategic Human Resources Management. There is an indisputable influence of the shadow economy on the employment situation in an economy. The shadow economy increases the unemployment in the official sector. On the other hand, new jobs in the underground economy are created. Some of the instruments of combating the shadow economy like deregulation of labour markets, redistribution of work and working hours regulations are also relevant with regards to HRM.
Business Law	Which law areas are touched by the proposals? What has to be done to make the proposals law safe?	Numerous initiatives and sanctions of the German government, the EU Commission and EU Parliament attempt to contain illicit work. To be mentioned is for example the German "Gesetz zur Bekämpfung der Schwarzarbeit und illegalen Beschäftigung".

Main Topic	Reasonable Questions	Recommendations/Comments
Research Methods / Management Decision Making	Which information source should be used, to bring keep the topic up-to-date? Which criteria should be used do decide for the right options?	There are several information sources and literature on the topic. However, many of them concentrate just on one single aspect of the phenomenon of the shadow economy, e.g. illicit work. Furthermore, the attempts to quantify the shadow economy should be taken with a pinch of salt as obtaining accurate statistics information and exact figures about the extent of the shadow economy is difficult. The gathered data is often based on estimations and indirect measuring approaches.
Soft Skills / Leadership	Which demands takes place on the responsible managers to realize the proposals? Which leadership concept is the appropriate?	An effective containment of illicit work and tax evasion poses a serious challenge for both, the government and general economy. Especially the leadership competence and strategic management skills of policy makers are required in order to elaborate effective measures for limiting the shadow economy.

YOUR KNOWLEDGE HAS VALUE